How Can We Describe Weather?

HOUGHTON MIFFLIN HARCOURT

PHOTOGRAPHY CREDITS: COVER ©Getty Images Royalty Free; 5 (br) ©vblinov/ Shutterstock; 6 (tl) ©Getty Images Royalty Free; 6 (cl) © Gene Blevins/LA DailyNews/Corbis; 6 (tr) ©G.K./Shutterstock; 6 (cr) Comstock/Getty Images; 6 (br) ©Keith Leighton/Alamy; 7 (bc) ©Digital Vision/Getty Images; 7 (bl) Paul Pegler/Alamy; 7 (br) ©Getty Images; 9 (br) ©Serge Krouglikoff/Digital Vision/ Getty Images; 11 (b) ©Jupiterimages/Getty Images; 12 (r) ©Simon Belcher/ Alamy; 13 ©Corbis; 14 (b) ©Weatherstock/Corbis; 15 (tr) ©Alamy Images

Printed in U.S.A.

ISBN: 978-0-544-07275-6

3 4 5 6 7 8 9 10 1083 21 20 19 18 17 16 15 14

4500470073   A B C D E F G

Be an Active Reader!

Look for each word in yellow along with its meaning.

weather	fresh water	water cycle
atmosphere	evaporation	temperature
oxygen	condensation	
salt water	precipitation	

Underlined sentences answer these questions.

What is weather?

What is the atmosphere?

What kind of water do we have on Earth?

What are the three forms of water?

What is evaporation?

How are clouds formed?

What is condensation?

What is the water cycle?

What is temperature?

How does temperature affect precipitation?

How can we measure wind and rainfall?

What is a meteorologist?

What is weather?

Pretend that you are talking to someone on the phone. The person asks you this question: "How's your weather today?"

You could probably answer that question. You already know that weather is about rain and snow. It is about how hot or cold it is outside. It is about the air! Weather is what is happening in the air at a certain time and place.

What words would you use to describe the weather outside this window?

What is the atmosphere?

There is a name for the air around our planet. It is called the atmosphere. Our atmosphere is made up of a mixture of gases. The atmosphere protects us. Without it, we would be too hot during the day. We would freeze at night.

One of the gases in Earth's atmosphere is oxygen. People and animals need oxygen to live.

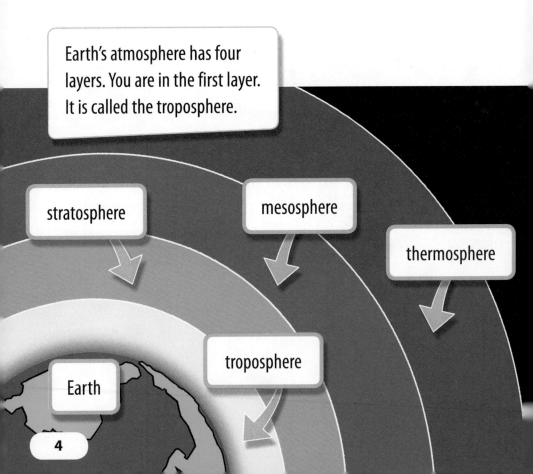

Earth's atmosphere has four layers. You are in the first layer. It is called the troposphere.

stratosphere

mesosphere

thermosphere

troposphere

Earth

What kind of water do we have on Earth?

There is salt water and fresh water on Earth. Salt water fills the oceans and seas. Drinking salt water will make you sick.

Fresh water has very little salt in it. It's the kind of water we drink. When water goes into the atmosphere, it leaves the salt behind. Water in the atmosphere is fresh.

The amount of water in the air is called humidity. The humidity changes from day to day. You can measure the amount with a special instrument. It is called a hygrometer.

Humidity is the amount of water in the air. You can measure humidity with a hygrometer.

What are the three forms of water?

There are three forms of water: solid, liquid, and gas. All three forms affect the weather.

Solid water is ice. Snow, sleet, and hail are all solid water. When ice melts, it becomes liquid water. Rain and fog are both liquid water.

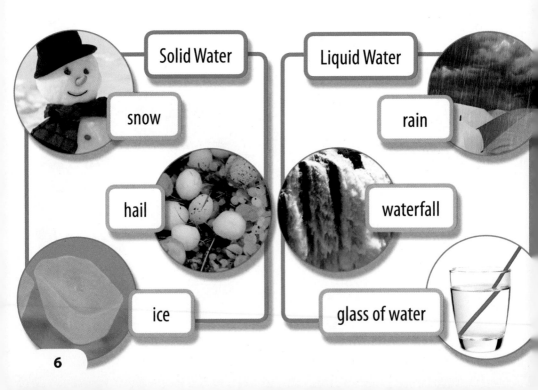

Solid Water

snow

hail

ice

Liquid Water

rain

waterfall

glass of water

What is evaporation?

Liquid water can turn into water vapor at low temperatures, too. The surface of water slowly turns into gas. That is called evaporation.

Try this! Take a washcloth and get it wet. Hang it up in the bathroom. Wait for a day. Then go and look at it again. Is it still wet? No! That's because the water evaporated. It turned into gas and went into the air.

Water on the surface of our oceans, lakes, and rivers evaporates into the air.

How are clouds formed?

When water evaporates, it becomes an invisible gas in the sky. Then it cools. It can turn back into liquid or it can freeze and become visible. Clouds form. Clouds are made of tiny droplets of water or ice. Clouds can tell us what kind of weather to expect.

Close to Earth's surface, a stratus cloud might form. Stratus clouds look like thin blankets. They can mean that it will rain or snow. Cumulus clouds are close to Earth's surface, too. They look like cotton. These clouds can mean that the weather will be fair. Cirrus clouds form higher in the atmosphere. Cirrus clouds can mean that the weather will change.

Clouds form when evaporated water in the air turns back into liquid water or ice. Each kind can tell us something about the weather.

cirrus

cumulus

stratus

What is condensation?

Condensation is the opposite of evaporation. Condensation is the change of water vapor into liquid water.

Did you ever pour very cold water into a glass on a hot day? If so, you probably saw drops of water form on the outside of the glass. The water vapor in the air turned into liquid water when it touched the cold glass. That is condensation.

Water vapor is in the air. When it touches cold glass, it becomes liquid.

What is the water cycle?

The movement of water from Earth to the air and back again is called the water cycle.

In the water cycle, water 1) evaporates, 2) condenses, 3) falls as rain and snow, and then 4) sinks back into the ground. The cycle repeats over and over again.

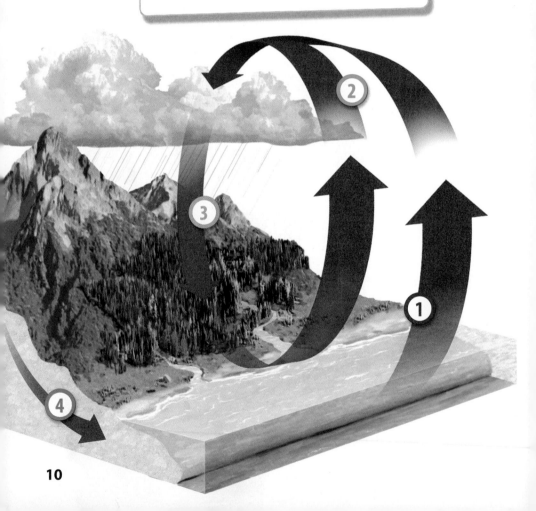

1. The sun heats water in the ocean and other places. As it warms, the water evaporates. It becomes water vapor. The water vapor rises into the air. It mixes with other gases.

2. As the water vapor rises, it cools. It condenses into water droplets or freezes into ice crystals. This makes clouds.

3. Next, the water falls back to Earth. This is called precipitation. Precipitation can be in the form of rain, sleet, snow, or hail.

4. Some water falls into the ocean. Some falls onto dry land. That water may sink into the ground. It may flow into rivers and streams. Rivers and streams flow back to the ocean.

The sun is a star. It is close to Earth. Its energy keeps the water cycle going.

What is temperature?

Weather is the temperature, precipitation, and wind in an area. Temperature is a measure of how hot or cold something is.

We measure temperature with a thermometer. This thermometer has a glass tube with red liquid inside. Numbers next to the tube show the temperature.

We use two different ways of numbering degrees. One is degrees Celsius (°C). The other is degrees Fahrenheit (°F).

23 °C

74 °F

°C °F

50 — 120
40 — 100
30 — 80
20 — 60
10 — 40
0 — 20
10 — 0
20 — 20
30 —

The thermometer shows one temperature. 23 °C is the same as 74 °F.

To find the temperature, look for the line next to the top of the liquid. Read the thermometer on page 12. What is the temperature in degrees Fahrenheit (°F)? What is the temperature in degrees Celsius (°C)?

Air temperature can change a lot. A place can be very hot at one time of year. But at another time, that same place can be very cold.

Look at the chart below. What are the highest and lowest temperatures in degrees Celsius? What are the highest and lowest temperatures in degrees Fahrenheit?

In Houston, Texas, summers are very hot. Winters can be cold, too!

Houston, Texas	°F	°C
Highest temperature recorded	104	40
Lowest temperature recorded	10	−12

How does temperature affect precipitation?

There are many forms of precipitation. There are rain, sleet, snow, and hail. Temperature affects the form of precipitation that we get.

Some precipitation is made up of more than one form of water. Sleet is frozen or partly frozen rain. It is caused by changes in temperature as rain falls. Hailstones are made when layers of liquid water freeze on top of each other.

Rain usually falls when the air is above 0 °C (32 °F). When the air is below 0 °C (32 °F), snow, sleet, or hail may fall.

Look closely at this hailstone. You can see the layers of ice that made it.

How can we measure wind and rainfall?

Wind is moving air. Weather scientists want to know two things about wind: its direction and its speed. A wind vane shows what direction the wind is blowing. A wind meter tells how fast the wind is blowing. Wind makes cups on a wind meter spin. Scientists measure how fast the cups spin to find out the wind speed.

A wind meter measures how fast the wind is blowing.

We measure rainfall with a rain gauge. A rain gauge collects rain in a tube with numbers.

Look at this rain gauge. Find the top of the water line. What number is it close to? That is how many inches of rain have fallen.

A rain gauge shows how much rain has fallen.

What is a meteorologist?

A meteorologist [MEE·tee·u·RAHL·uh·jist] is a person who studies weather and reports on it. Weather reports help us decide what to wear, where to go, and what to do.

Meteorologists also tell us about what the weather is going to be like in coming days. This helps us to make plans. We can plan a picnic outside on a day when it will not rain.

Some kinds of weather can be dangerous. Heat waves, thunderstorms, tornadoes, and hurricanes are examples. Weather reports help us plan for these kinds of weather. We can decide what to do to stay safe.

Meteorologists study the atmosphere. They can tell us about the weather.

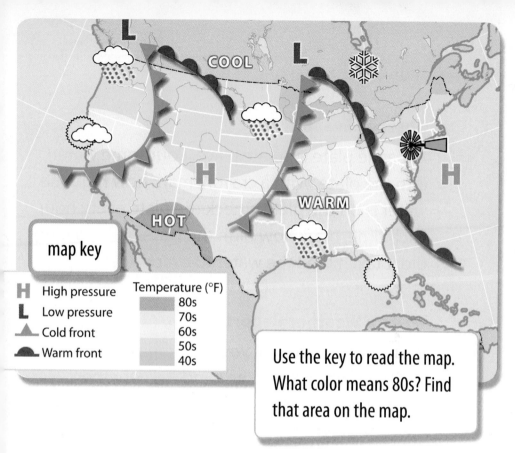

map key

		Temperature (°F)
H	High pressure	80s
L	Low pressure	70s
▲ Cold front		60s
● Warm front		50s
		40s

Use the key to read the map. What color means 80s? Find that area on the map.

Meteorologists also tell us about weather in different places. They use a weather map like the one above to show this information. The map has a key to show how to read it.

Observe Evaporation

Put a pie plate in a safe place. Pour some water into the plate. With a crayon, mark how high the water is on the plate. Check the plate every hour. Each time, mark how high the water is. How long did it take for all the water to evaporate?

Write a Weather Report

Write a description of your weather. Describe the temperature and the wind. Tell whether there is precipitation. If there is, tell what kind. Say whether the sky is clear or cloudy. Say what people could do in this kind of weather. For example, is this a good day for a picnic? Is it a good day to sit inside and read a book?

Glossary

atmosphere [AT·muhs·feer] The layer of gases that surround Earth. *The atmosphere around Earth is different from the atmosphere around Mars.*

condensation [kahn·duhn·SAY·shuhn] The process by which a gas changes into a liquid. *Condensation left dew on the morning grass.*

evaporation [ee·vap·uh·RAY·shuhn] The process by which a liquid changes into a gas. *Evaporation left the street dry after a rain.*

fresh water [FRESH WAW·ter] Water that has very little salt in it. *Some turtles live only in fresh water.*

oxygen [OK·si·jen] A gas in the air and water, which most living things need to survive. *Oxygen is in the air we breathe.*

precipitation [pri·sip·uh·TAY·shuhn] Water that falls from clouds to Earth's surface. *Most of the precipitation that falls in a rain forest is rain.*

salt water [SAWLT WAW·ter] Water found in oceans and seas; makes up 97% of Earth's water. *Penguins can drink salt water, but most animals cannot.*

temperature [TEM•per•uh•cher] A measure of how hot or cold something is. *The air was cool today, but the temperature will be warm tomorrow.*

water cycle [WAW•ter SY•kuhl] The movement of water from Earth's surface to the air and back again. *Sam drew the sun, clouds, and the ocean in this picture of the water cycle.*

weather [WETH•er] What is happening in the atmosphere at a certain place and time. *The weather has been snowy and cold all week.*